ANTONI
Gaudí

To the Bodington household
and to Samuel on his sixth birthday

THIS IS A CARLTON BOOK

Text and design copyright © 1999 Carlton Books Limited

This edition published by Carlton Books Limited 1999
20 St Anne's Court
Wardour Street
London
W1V 3AW

A CIP catalogue for this book is available from the British Library

ISBN 1 85868 747 0

EXECUTIVE EDITOR: Sarah Larter
MANAGING ART EDITOR: Zoë Mercer
DESIGN: Simon Mercer
PICTURE RESEARCH: Alex Pepper
PRODUCTION: Garry Lewis

Printed and bound in Dubai

ANTONI
Gaudí

Visionary Architect of the Sacred and the Profane

JUDITH CARMEL-ARTHUR

CARLTON

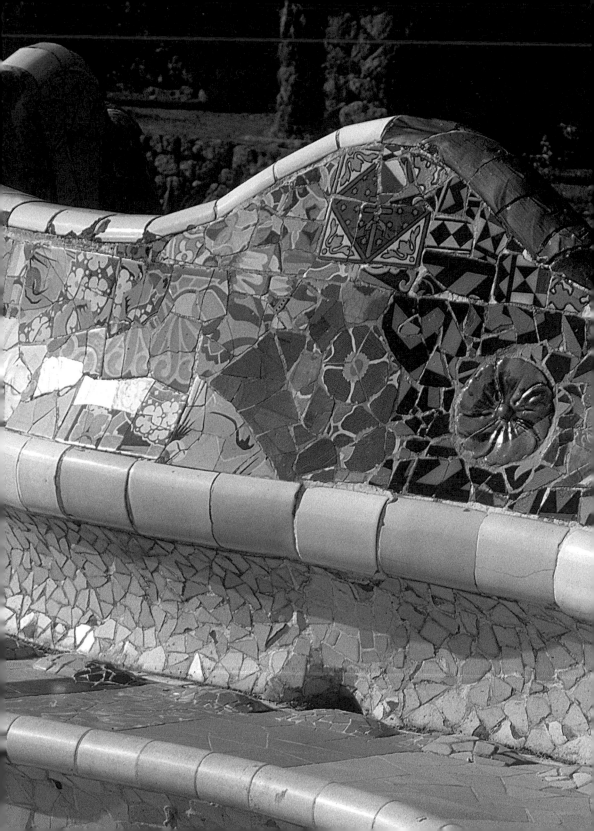

Gaudí

— designer of residential spaces characterized by an inestimable *fin-de-siècle* "pleasure principle", and religious edifices of haunting solemnity and complexion. A man whose legendary life, works and even death were marked by extremes, Gaudí has been trumpeted as a genius and equally demonized by critics, writers and journalists of the twentieth century. Whether visionary or viper, Gaudí left behind an architectural legacy that continues to generate controversy in the final decades of this century, while his devotional, even iconic appeal within his native Catalonia has not noticeably decreased during the nearly 80 years since his bizarre death in Barcelona in 1926. On the contrary, in late 1998 the Cardinal of Barcelona nominated Gaudí for sainthood, proposing his beatification on the basis of a "profound and constant contemplation of the mysteries of the faith".

Both architectural and popular literature have contributed to Gaudí's apotheosis as the foremost patriarch of Catalan cultural heritage. Even within his own lifetime he was stereotyped as a mad architectural genius and has since, in essence, been mythologized either as saint or subversive.

"**Death** CAME UPON GAUDÍ SUDDENLY, ONE AFTERNOON HE WAS WALKING, AS WAS HIS CUSTOM, TO THE CHURCH OF SAINT FELIP NERI TO PRAY, WHEN HE WAS run over BY A TRAM ... BECAUSE OF HIS RAGGED APPEARANCE HE WAS NOT RECOGNIZED OR GIVEN THE EMERGENCY TREATMENT HE REQUIRED" LLUIS PERMANYER

A N T O N I

The very language of the Gaudí myth – that is, the myth's "text" – effectively embodies this polemic, revealing the extent to which we culturally link notions of fame, suffering and creativity in the portrayal of our artistic celebrities. Perceptions of Gaudí have been cloaked beneath a Janus-like garment of notoriety in our desire to understand his magical, fairy tale buildings which – rather like his life – conjure up impressions of sanity on one level, psychosis beneath; the sacred and the profane.

"THE THINGS THAT **HAVEN'T CHANGED** ARE THE PLODDING ONWARDS-AND-UPWARDS **construction** OF GAUDÍ'S SAGRADA FAMILIA" JONATHAN GLANCEY, ARCHITECTURAL CRITIC

Recently Gaudí's work has been highlighted internationally during Barcelona's widespread urban renewal for the 1992 Olympic Games, and by the city's reception of the prestigious Royal Institute of British Architects' Gold Medal in March 1999. Despite the extensive renovation and redevelopment, however, one question of civic importance within Barcelona remains concerning Gaudí's *magnum opus* and "extraordinary stone vegetable patch", the Church of the Sagrada Familia – "But what of the cathedral?"

G A U D Í

The Sacred

Referred to mockingly as a "pile of stones", construction began on the Expiatory Temple of the Holy Family in 1882 and was entrusted to the 31-year-old Gaudí as early as November 1883. Prior to this Gaudí had completed no major independent architectural commission, although his first residential commission in Barcelona, the Casa Vicens (1878–1888), was well underway. During 1882 he had worked alongside the medievalist Catalan architect Joan Martorell i Montells, under whose auspices he learnt an eclectic formulation of revivalist idioms in the popular neo-Gothic style. The younger architect's potential was clearly manifest, for it was with Martorell's endorsement in the following year that Gaudí obtained the esteemed post of Director of Works at the immense Basilica of the Holy Family.

Gaudí's supervision of the cathedral programme lasted for 43 years to 1926. Among the best-known anecdotes of Gaudí's life is that he resided in modest workshops in the cathedral precinct during his final years: a decision no doubt dictated by a combination of logistical convenience, the effects of increasing ill health and his fervent devotion to the realization of this monumental and enigmatic shrine. Such an apparently idiosyncratic gesture confirms the depths to which Gaudí had entrenched himself within a crafts ideology, if not an historicist allure of great past traditions of Medieval cathedral building.

> "THIS IS THE **last** IMPERIOUS **monument** OF CATHOLIC **SPAIN**"
>
> ROBERT HUGHES, *THE SHOCK OF THE NEW*

Born in Reus, Spain in 1852, Gaudí was trained as a craftsman in ornamental and utilitarian copperwork and metal smithing by his father. His natural orientation towards a very direct, hands-on approach to both the designing and making processes was well suited to his future architectural profession. It positioned him felicitously within the romantic and political ideologies of Catalonia's late nineteenth-century cultural resurgence movement, the *Renaixença*, of which both Barcelona and Gaudí were quickly at the heart.

Even within that cosmopolitan port and industrial city, the cathedral precinct was itself conceived as the nucleus of a small "suburb" populated by sculpture and stone-cutting workshops, in addition to model-making studios and even a parish school that still survives.

The complexity of the programme required a multiplicity of master craftsmen and engineers performing as a unified team committed to Gaudí's architectural agenda. Within their midst Gaudí himself is said to have scurried about attending to every manner of structural, engineering and aesthetic detail. The fulfilment of the undertaking, then, was not strictly weighted upon his shoulders – the notoriously fanatical, mad genius of art historical myth – but remained dependent upon established architectural traditions of expertise and multidisciplinary endeavour.

All too often overlooked, this is well worth highlighting for despite the defiantly carcass-like embryo of the church, Gaudí bequeathed to Barcelona a legacy of co-operative workmanship to which generations of craftsmen like him have devoutly contributed. Historically, the cathedral has been heralded not exclusively as Gaudí's endeavour, but in a more nationalistic vein as that of all Catalans, invoking John Ruskin's deeply romantic espousal of the authority of medieval architectural practice with its intimate brotherhood of masons, cutters, pavers, tilers, glaziers and sculptors working in tandem with the local community, dedicated en masse to actualizing an architectural and devotional ideology intrinsically linked to the tangible, economic well-being of the their "extended" community.

> **"THE NECESSARY CONSEQUENCE OF THIS ENTHUSIASM IN USEFUL BUILDINGS, WAS THE FORMATION OF A VAST BODY OF craftsemen AND ARCHITECTS ... THEIR PERSONAL CHARACTER WAS FOUNDED ON THE ACCURATE KNOWLEDGE OF THEIR BUSINESS IN ALL RESPECTS ... COUPLED WITH A GENERAL CONTENTMENT IN LIFE AND IN ITS VIGOUR AND SKILL"**
>
> JOHN RUSKIN, *VAL D'ARNO*, LECTURE III

Gaudí's sympathies with the sociological dogma of John Ruskin's Arts and Crafts ideology, which he had studied, help to illuminate the allure of the crafts-orientated, communal ambience of the cathedral precinct where he was able to focus his abilities ensconced within meagre studio quarters.

Gaudí saw the near completion of only one of three main façades of the church – the eastern Nativity façade; three of four eastern towers, less their kaleidoscopic, ceramic-encrusted pinnacles which were then finished almost immediately following his death; the crypt begun in 1882 by the first architect Francesc de Paula Villar i Lozano and completed to the latter's design; and a substantial segment of the outer apse wall. The building thereafter remained a masonry casing, more fantastic in its visual appeal by virtue of its motiveless and fragmentary state.

As a church of atonement, resources for the new cathedral were insufficient from the outset. Never receiving municipal assistance, the church was to be constructed entirely from the private sector by donations, some of which Gaudí himself solicited on foot in Barcelona during the First World War.

Sons and grandsons of craftsmen who worked there with Gaudí continue a resolute familial association with the controversial, but perpetually unfinished project. These include the architect Jordi Bonet, an outspoken advocate of Barcelona's commitment to realizing Gaudí's plans. His advocacy today is pitted against an opposition – formerly boasting as advocates the so-called fathers of architectural Modernism, Walter Gropius and Le Corbusier – which has consistently petitioned to suspend work on the cathedral, arguing that additions in the aftermath of Gaudí's death are, at best, imitations or, at worst, kitsch.

Gaudí's church remains inflected towards the neo-Gothic idioms of his early career only in its emphatic height and ideological purpose. The cathedral's first architect, Villar, was

"HERE ONE CAN **TRUTHFULLY** SAY THAT **form** DOES FOLLOW **function** – SLIDING, DRIPPING, DISSOLVING, RE-FORMING, CHANGING COLOUR AND **TEXTURE**; SOFT ARCHITECTURE, JUICY ARCHITECTURE, THE ARCHITECTURE OF **ecstasy**"

ROBERT HUGHES, *THE SHOCK OF THE NEW*

responsible for the conventional Latin Cross plan and overall disposition. The building's imposing proportions are meant to harbour five naves, the central one measuring a formidable 95 metres in length, with the transept length two-thirds of that and 30 metres across. It's choir galleries could ideally accommodate a daunting 1500 vocalists and perhaps 7 pipe organs.

However, Gaudí inaugurated an increasingly dramatic rejection of any historicizing neo-Gothic approach, contradicting his own youthful influences and re-presenting with imagination the traditional typology for a basilican church.

"LIKE A **gigantic** DECAYED TOOTH, FULL OF **POSSIBILITIES**"

— SALVADOR DALI ON THE SAGRADA FAMILIA

Gaudí's training had essentially been an inculcation into neo-Gothicism. As an architectural student at Barcelona's Escuela Superior he became immersed in the popular stylistic approach of Barcelona's most persuasive medieval revivalist architects. He was subsequently exposed to the ethical medievalism of Joan Martorell, and worked with Villar on a neo-Romanesque chapel at Montserrat Monastery. During this period Gaudí also assiduously read Violett le Duc's neo-Gothic theories of structural rationalism in the recently published *Entretiens sur l'Architecture*.

Nevertheless, his two early buildings considered the "most" neo-Gothic merely bow to medieval styling on their exteriors and in some internal features. Both the Bishop's Palace, Astorga (commissioned 1887) and the commercial-cum-residential Casa de los Botines (1881–84) use neo-Gothic elements with sophisticated economy, such as tripartite glazing, corner turrets, pointed arches, French Gothic capitals and rounded towers. Motifs drawn from medieval secular precedents also appear and are combined by Gaudí in a thoroughly eclectic fashion. These buildings prove Gaudí's intimacy with medievalist styling and suggest the neo-Gothic typology which might have been used at the Sagrada Familia, but wasn't.

His novel treatment of the eastern Nativity façade, surmounted by those looming parabolic bell towers, which measure approximately 100 metres each, is anything but conventional. This is not only the most photographed section of the existing building, but provides the most tangible evidence of Gaudí's mature, increasingly aberrant architectural vision.

Gaudí's animated and interpenetrating surfaces confirm his interpretation of architecture as organic structure which expresses the growth potential and evolutionary properties of nature. As Rainer Zerbst has pointed out, "For Gaudí, however, nature consisted of forces that work beneath the surface, which was merely an expression of these inner forces. For example, he studied how stone blocks behaved when placed under pressure by putting them in a hydraulic press." The façade of Sagrada Familia is a purposeful visual statement of this architectural approach, and parallels the equally geological, but more tentative "jagged" undulations of his Casa Batlló (1904–1906,) and the broader, more intrepid triple façades of the famously "cliff-like" Casa Milá (1906–1910).

On all three buildings Gaudí looked upon the rock-coloured faces as opportunities to meld sculptural plasticity with architectural mass; to the extent that it becomes impossible to see where one structural or decorative element ends and the next begins.

The enormous bell towers equally defy comparison with any architectural precedents outside of Gaudí's own oeuvre. Initially conceived as square, with Gaudí they evolved into rounded, majestic protuberances. Their tapering, futuristic appearance does not derive from antecedent Gothic spires, but rather from their idiosyncratic parabolic configurations, complemented by an open network of square and columnar braces producing a honeycombed effect. Their aggressive upward thrust acutely expresses Gaudí's predilection for growth metaphors, the labyrinth of towers suggesting an otherworldly "forest in stone".

Similarly, figural sculpture depicting Biblical scenes and meant to adorn the cathedral throughout fulfilled not only a conventional didactic purpose, but also symbolic and metaphorical ones. Based by Gaudí upon a series of plaster moulds and photographs taken from living models, their implicit human fragility must be understood to be juxtaposed to the intrinsic, elemental brutality of the façade's pulsating surface.

The architect clearly intended the visual messages of the new cathedral to be read in different ways and on a number of different levels as "cultural" language. In addition to architectural, symbolic, and metaphorical imagery, he also adapted textual inscriptions to the fabric of the building. In so doing he identified the cathedral entity as an adroit amalgamation of text and image; a result of the pairing of his somewhat raw creativity with his erudite and zealous religiosity.

The Sagrada Familia is not so unlike most of Gaudí's other architectural projects in that it defies stylistic categorization. Nevertheless, it does have precedents within his own oeuvre which also show an exquisite interplay between surface, space and structure, setting the stage for the success of his daring innovations at the Sagrada Famila.

The parabolic arch, one of Gaudí's most notorious personal trademarks, is worth focusing upon here, for although it appeared in both his secular and religious buildings, it is likely to have been developed for not only its structural efficiency, but to provoke an atmosphere of the sacred rather than the secular.

His experimentation with its potential may have begun as early as 1882, its first proper appearance was in the stables of the Güell Pavillions (1887) where it facilitated the infusion of soft natural light through the arched openings in the roof.

At about the same time at the Palau Güell (1887–91) in Barcelona Gaudí confidently manipulated the parabola as a significant engineering, as well as theatrical feature in a residential setting of some magnificence. Here, the parabolic arch appears in two ways: firstly, in twin arches of the entrance, and on bay windows above; secondly, as the main structural element creating the apparently monumental interior spaces grouped about the reception area covered by the substantial parabolic vaulting.

With the Colegio Teresiano, Barcelona (1889–94) Gaudí achieved a breathtaking degree of spatial and architectural abstraction in the internal hallways of this motherhouse of the Order of St. Theresa of Avila. Here the parabolic arch is handled as the foremost architectural motif of the interior. The poetic temperament of its configuration and its ability to accommodate consecutively windowed curtain walls without the use of heavy, external buttressing being exploited to create an atmosphere of meditative calm entirely appropriate to the setting.

The most dramatic precedents for the forceful treatment of the parabola at the Sagrada Familia, however, are in some especially fantastic plans for two unexecuted projects, both known today through drawings.

The earliest of these (1892–93) sketches was for a church and monastery for the Franciscans of Tangier, and reveals the beginnings of Gaudí's ideas for the cluster of parabolic towers used subsequently at the Sagrada Familia. Then in 1908 he sketched remarkably similar ideas for a hotel complex in New York City, again boasting groups of parabolic towers perhaps 200 to 300 metres in height. These towers are simply the silhouette of the parabolic arch twisted 360 degrees, resulting in "rotational parabolas" whose true symbolic meaning still remains unclear.

While working on the mature phases of the Sagrada Famila, Gaudí was simultaneously engaged on another important commission for sacred structures: the unrealized Chapel and incomplete Crypt (1898–1917) of the Güell Colony in Sant Coloma de Cervelló. Gaudí's surviving drawings clearly suggest the church was envisaged as the fruition of the parabolic tower groupings imagined for the New York and Tangiers projects. Revealingly, or perhaps fortuitously, no project including this disconcerting feature was ever built and – although the towers are noticeably narrower – those of the Sagrada Familia are not complete nearly 100 years later. But for the small chapel planned for the Park Güell, this is only the second church of Gaudí's career.

The Güell Colony Crypt, however, is extraordinary. Its slanting columns and arcuated structures disable conventional perceptions of interior space and architectural support. But for the exquisite craftsmanship of the brick- and basaltwork and the sophisticated arrangement of the many polychromed, ceramic surfaces, the crypt gives the impression of having been excavated from slanted fissures in the hillock of which it forms an organic part.

Within the crypt Gaudí excells in his gifts as a structural engineer. It is impossible not to enthusiastically praise such an enchanting and yet brutal spiritual space where the altar chapel ceiling suddenly proliferates in a cage of primitive arches and columns which seem to be driven by centrifugal force.

The unprecedented eccentricity of the structure is consistent with that of the Park Güell of about the same time. Both betray a symbiosis between architecture and nature that marks Gaudí's mature eclectic style and his increasingly confident subversion of established canons of form and function. His favouring of nature as the fundamental frame of reference for the invention of both symbolism and structure is extreme, while his expression of raw, unrefined power in form, texture, materials and space in concert divorces his work from superficial, populist expressions of Art Nouveau in both Barcelona and northern Europe. What Gaudí does have in common with "Art Nouveau" practitioners is his harmonious synthesis of multiple materials, and both craftswork and architectural expression into a unique, unified whole in the manner of the Gesamtkunstwerk – the "total work of art". This approach, so evident in the Güell Colony Crypt, is most apparent in his residential schemes.

The Secular

Gaudí was born a Catalan. During his formative years as an architectural student in Barcelona from 1869 to 1878 he witnessed the strengthening of the city's umbrella nationalist movement which included both regionalists and separatists, and here developed the fervent Catalan sympathies that characterized his life and career. In Barcelona's architectural culture he was at the vanguard of the nationalist sentiment shared by the majority of leading Catalan architects including Francisco del Villar, Martorell, Lluis Domènech i Montaner, and Puig i Cadafalch, whose largely regionalist ideology even infiltrated Gaudí's education at the Escuela Superior de Arquitectura where he matriculated in 1878. He belonged to study groups such as the Centre Excursionista who journeyed to Catalonia's historic monuments, perceived as icons of the region's glorious past and whose study would inspire the assertion of national identity.

Two of Gaudí's earliest jobs carried further undertones of the ideology of the Catalan cultural resurgence movement known as the *Renaixença*. Joining Villar at work on a neo-Romanesque chapel at Montserrat in 1877, he worked briefly within an architectural style promoted amongst "national" idioms by *Renaixença* protagonists. In the following year he exhibited preparatory drawings in Paris for a new settlement comprising residential facilities and a factory for the co-operative of textile artisans at Mataro; a programme betraying Renaixença ideology in its paternalistic sentiment and the influence of John Ruskin's social ideology. By the time Gaudí began his first independent architectural commission, the Casa Vicens in Barcelona in 1883, he was saturated with a pietistic utopianism that professed cultural resurgence and argued for a unification of the ancient with the contemporary as the means to a better future.

> "IN HIS **HEART** GAUDÍ ALWAYS REMAINED TRUE TO HIS **origins**. HE FELT CLOSE TO THE COMMON **PEOPLE**"

RAINER ZERBST

In his secular commissions Gaudí willingly provoked issues of his Catalan identity. In his hands materials and motifs were used symbolically to invite reminiscences of Catalan culture.

The major secular monuments dating from his earliest period as an independent architect in the 1880s are qualified by their eclectic stylistic approach, but all show his ability to communicate political and social meaning through the visual vocabulary of architecture and decoration. Buildings such as the Casa Vicens (1883–88), the rural villa "El Capricho" (the "caprice", "whim"; 1883–85) and the remarkably elegant Güell Pavilions (1884–87) with their latticework of honeycombed stucco are well known for their expression of a "Moorish", but more accurately *Mudèjar* style at which Gaudí became an acknowledged master.

The *Mudèjar* style, an art and architecture of Islamic derivation arising on the Iberian Peninsula in the eleventh century, was revived during the late nineteenth century within a specifically Catalan context. It constituted a local re-elaboration of traditional forms, materials and techniques combining Christian with Arabic, Persian and North African elements in a hybrid style of decorative exuberance. It appeared in Gaudí's work and elsewhere as part of a synthetic, decorative approach at the vanguard of the Catalan medievalist revival, which also included the neo-Gothic idiom. *Mudèjar* motifs became signals particularly of cultural entrenchment and, as such, were translated into a highly graceful and sophisticated form of visual propaganda.

The exteriors of Gaudí's buildings named above are thoroughly indicative of his mannered interpretation of the *Mudèjar* style. The crowning minaret-like turrets recollect indigenous Islamic tradition; in their largely decorative rather than functional purpose becoming leitmotifs in Gaudí's oeuvre. The tower-minaret subsequently appears shamelessly upon his secular roof spaces which increasingly become plateaux for expressive, sometimes even subversive architectural form, such as at the Palau Güell, and most dramatically later at the Casas Batlló and Milá

A *Mudèjar* inflection is also seen in Gaudí's proclivity towards dense surface ornamentation and patterning, created by horizontal and stepped detailing of decorative brickwork and finely polychromed, ceramic cladding. At the Casa Vicens these features also make a very public statement about the patron who was an affluent brick and ceramic tile manufacturer, suggesting Gaudí's discriminating combination of design and craft was meant to help define, perhaps with political overtones, public perception of Barcelona's *haute bourgeoisie*.

An expressive and cosmopolitan use of polychromed ceramic tiling became one of Gaudí's stylistic trademarks, suggesting a personal penchant for crafts-based media. A consistently strong emphasis on materials in his work betrays his intrinsic understanding of craftsmanship and crafts-based methods as being at the very heart of good design. In this, he was a man of his time in Barcelona where a prominent crafts resurgence was fuelled by the desire to reassert past indigenous tradition.

Gaudí's Catalanist ideals were perhaps most in sympathy with those of his most important patron, the Catalan industrialist and paternalist, the Baron Eusebi Güell I Bacigalupi. He first met Güell in 1878 and would go on to design some of his most persuasive structures for this patron. Over 20 years, Güell commissioned from Gaudí a series of substantial projects, their authority and sheer creative drive attesting to the intimate and nurturing bond between architect and patron.

" [HE WAS THE] **most** CATALONIAN OF ALL **Catalonians** "

JOAQUIM TORRES GARCIA

These included the Güell Pavilions outside of Barcelona (1884–87), the Palau Güell (1886–89), the Crypt and Chapel of the Colonia Güell (1898–1917), modest warehouses and a chapel at the Bodegas Güell, Garraf (1895–1905), and the checkerboard-like Park Güell (1900–14) overlooking Barcelona.

With Güell, Gaudí became ever more ensconced within Catalan cultural politics. At his patron's home he met with other avant-garde and romanticist artists, poets and novelists of the *Renaixença* movement, discussing among other topics the reformist writings of John Ruskin and the French neo-Gothicist Viollet-le-Duc, both of whom advocated a regionalist approach to architecture. Clearly Güell saw himself as a new patron of the emerging Catalan arts, while his prominent position in Barcelona's *haute bourgeoisie* allowed him to construct a pattern of patronage using contemporary design as a mechanism of federalist conservatism and bourgeoisie authority. Essentially, he employed Gaudí as part of an aesthetic power base which derived from the political and paternalistic affinities shared between the two. Gaudí upheld the primacy of the architect as "divine artificer" in the formulation and betterment of contemporary Catalonia, while Güell used Gaudí to position himself at the forefront of paternal benefaction, making tangible his own self-righteous ideas about the bearing of Barcelona's industrially-based middle-classes.

During the 1890s both Gaudí and Güell were closely aligned with the Circol de Sant Lluch, a para-official, Catholic group of influence in Barcelona, composed of the artistic and educated who sought to renew urban society by means of an ideology based upon charity, artistry and morality. It boasted itself a guild of "Artisans of Beauty" referring to a pronounced crafts bias.

The Palau Güell (1886–91) is a palatial, grey-marble encrusted urban residence, also intended as a luxurious focus for *Renaixença* cultural activities. Its massive column between the entry portals of the ground storey exhibits the Catalan emblem. Built no doubt as a showcase for the forthcoming 1888 Barcelona World Exposition, the palace displays the patron's taste, aesthetic erudition, and political persuasion. It also exemplifies Gaudí's synthetic incorporation of elements from *Mudèjar*, Gothic and Renaissance sources fused into a thoroughly individual statement.

The interior spaces are distributed about a magnificent central space rising through two storeys and supported by a parabolic vault lit from small star-like punctures in the cupola. The central reception hall below, dedicated to drama, dance and musical performances as well as literary gatherings, is neither wide nor long, but overall feels enormous because of the vaulting, exhibiting Gaudí's tendency to exploit effects of Baroque illusionism.

The deceptively simple façade is punctuated by two archways containing a intricately woven wrought-iron lattice fabricated to include allusions to Gaudí's patron. Wrought-iron ornamentation was deeply indicative of Gaudí's aesthetic and allowed him to achieve an unlimited degree of self-expression via crafts-based skill. This is borne out early on in the delightful iron-work benches, arbours and little balconies of "El Capricho", and thereafter throughout his oeuvre.

The grandiose and prison-like "Dragon Gate" linking the two small Güell Pavillions is, however, one of Gaudí's greatest realizations of exotic fantasy in wrought-iron. Of ceremonial bearing, the gate gives access to a recreational estate. The dynamic tension of the design is equally two and three dimensional, relying on nervousness of line as much as texture. It displays a huge frightening dragon with splayed jaws and extended wings emerging from a twisted body. Defensive iron talons arise from the dragon's claw when the gate is opened; a not so subtle device of power and intimidation.

Gaudí's penultimate commission from Güell was for the chapel and crypt at the latter's model community with factory, housing for industrial textile workers and a school at the Güell Colony, Santa Coloma de Cervelló. Although only the crypt was built (1898–1917), the concept betrayed Catholic reactionism against encroaching effects of secularization, as well as Güell's paternalist motives which, again, Gaudí was called upon actualize.

A similar motivation inspired the Park Güell (1900–14), a landscape of extravagance nestled in the hills above Barcelona. This extensive park was equally meant to express Güell's confidence in the reformist ideology of the *Renaixença*. It was conceived by Gaudí as a "garden suburb" accommodating as many as sixty individual middle-class households in a walled community, complete with infrastructure such as viaducts, avenues, play area, covered market and plaza. Only two houses were built, while the church planned to symbolically arise from the summit of the hill was never constructed. The site is significant for its ennobled synthesis of the sacred and the secular, the spirit and the senses, the structural and the ornamental. In effect the Park Güell celebrated a middle-class "pleasure principle", underpinned by morality and family values, but nevertheless manifest in Gaudí's unprecedented fusion of texture, colour, natural and artificial space and structural form.

Still popular as municipal grounds, the Park Güell is at once impish and surrealistic; a fairytale garden combining the ethos of Disneyland with that of an anti-diluvian Jurassic Park. The site is circumscribed by serpentine enclosing walls setting the festive tenor of the recreational area within, while barring "the other" from outside the perimeter. Sloping walled grottoes excavated from the hillside, and columns and walls constructed of rough-hewn rubble introduce the concept that nature itself generates architectural form. A visible alliance with nature in repeated motifs of animals, plants, rocks and caves is complemented by arbitrary mosaic patternings which adorn the park's undulating structures. The polychromatic, tiled parapet-bench which effortlessly curls around the flat roof of the market hall is amongst the most famous examples of Gaudí's use of ceramic, porcelain and glass shards in abstract collages which also embellish fountains and a family of enigmatic sculpted pets. There can be little doubt that with this commission Gaudí firmly established his reputation as an eccentric genius.

The Profane

Park Güell was the start of a critical period of Gaudí's mature work in which conventional architecture decomposes and he conscientiously begins to subvert accepted norms of structural form and space.

The Casas Batlló and Milà represent the clearest assertion of Gaudí's mature organic style and are the pinnacle of his achievement in design for secular buildings. The buildings arose near one another in the heart of Barcelona, each comprising multiple rather than single apartments. They constitute highly self-assured architectural statements which were meant to be seen and meant to provoke.

The patrons of both buildings counted amongst Barcelona's industrial bourgeoisie for whom Gaudí redefined the very nature of an urban residence as a domestic utopia. In both instances the patrons clearly aspired to successfully compete within their milieu, making public declarations of architectural celebrity: therefore commissioning Eusebi Güell's architect. But for their origins in a regionalist, bourgeoisie ambience, both buildings would appear to be largely de-politicized, although the history of the Casa Milá was briefly touched by events of the *Semana Tragica*, the "Tragic Week", of July 1909.

During an episode of escalating anti-clericalism in Barcelona, the conservative Regionalist League, of which Gaudí and some of his patrons were members, provoked a violent repression of dissidents causing 83 demonstrators to die and some anarchists to face execution. In the aftermath, sculptural representations of the Virgin and Child, along with religious dedications planned for the façade of the Casa Milá were rejected by the patron.

The unprecedented absence of straight lines and right angles either inside or without the Casas Batlló and Milá have caused them to be consistently described by reference to biology, botany, geology and zoology – a virtual plethora of scientific and pseudo-scientific terminology used to explain what Gaudí himself called their thoroughly "anti-classical" and "anti-historicist" character.

Gaudí's intentional evocation not merely of nature, but more specifically of the emerging natural sciences is perhaps one of the most under-explored aspects of his architectural identity. During the late nineteenth century religion and science were still brimming with animosity. But in northern Europe a handful of exceptional Art Nouveau precursors and early practitioners combined a keen pursuit of the natural sciences with parallel careers in design. Among these, for example, the works of Arthur Heygate Mackmurdo and Christopher Dresser, a respected Doctor of Botany, would have been accessible to Gaudí through British Arts and Crafts sources such as *The Studio Magazine*. But it is somewhat less the point that their works embody osteomorphic linear swells and undulating organic surfaces as leitmotifs of the emerging Art Nouveau style, than that they acutely studied the natural sciences in and of themselves. In Mackmurdo's case, this also included the new social sciences as espoused in the evolutionary theory of, for example, Herbert Spencer.

"THE **wavy** FAÇADE, WITH ITS LARGE PORES, REMINDS ONE ALSO OF AN **UNDULATING BEACH** OF FINE SAND ... THE HONEYCOMBS MADE BY **industrious** BEES ..."

RAINER ZERBST

Gaudí had unquestionably looked directly at artefacts of the natural sciences, perhaps at Barcelona's new science museum, or in populist but influential, illustrated science publications such as those of Ernst Haeckel.

His visual – not architectural – language in the Casas Batlló and Milá was drawn from palaeontological, as well as geological sources. At the Casa Batlló this is patently apparent in the fossil-like column of vertebra, which appear to remain implanted within the rock-like stratum of the stairway. At the Casa Milá the cave-like articulation of windows and interior spaces betrays a similarly scientific tone, which in part then belies the steady claims that Gaudí's mature works, but for the excellence of their engineering, amount to nothing more than the musings of a madman.

Gaudí imitated such natural forms in order to create hybrid architectural statements, but because he rarely outright quoted the whole form of any organism, fossil or mineral aggregate it would perhaps be unsound to suggest he studied materials of the natural sciences in minute detail. Furthermore, because he refuses to quote "the whole", there is a feeling of things being only "partial". This imparts to his work associations with the "grotesque, fantastic, and chimeric", especially in his recollections of marine organisms.

The sculptural tendencies in both buildings is equally pronounced, confirming Gaudí's complete transition to a conceiving of architecture as lithe plastic form rather than immovable structure. Both buildings, but especially the Casa Milá visually move of their own accord, pushing the tensile strength of materials to its very limit. By this time in his career, Gaudí had come to approach architecture – both religious and secular – as the incarnation of evolutionary theory, dependent upon laws of nature which dictate that all life, all structure, is in constant transition. Surely, he has found a means of reconciling religion with science; the sacred with the profane.

"LET US **consider** WHAT IT MEANS TO BE **born** IN THE **MEDITERRANEAN** ... CATALANS HAVE A **NATURAL** SENSE OF (THE) **three-dimensional** THAT GIVES THEM AN IDEA OF THINGS AS A **WHOLE** AND OF THE RELATIONSHIP AMONG THINGS."

GAUDÍ

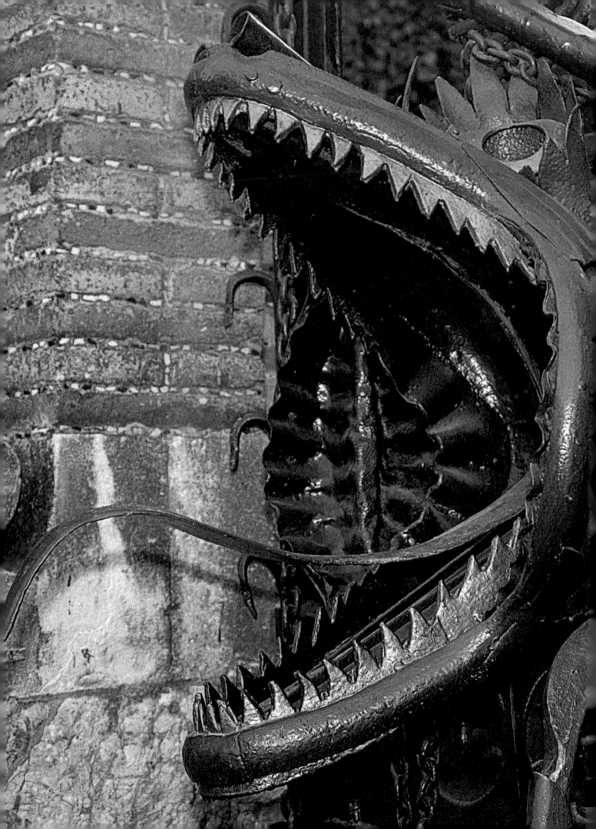

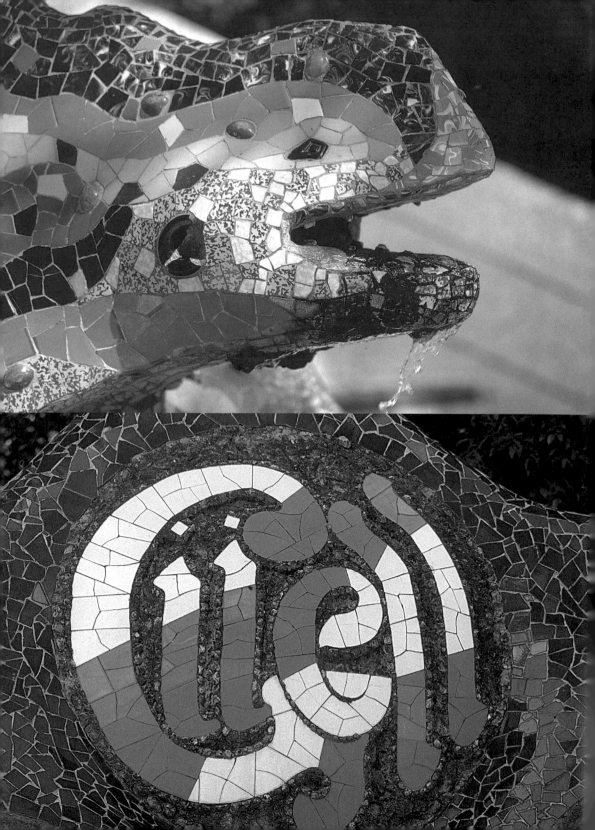

EXPIATORY TEMPLE OF THE HOLY FAMILY, THE "SAGRADA FAMILIA", 1883–1926

Barcelona. Bell towers of the eastern façade, adorned with polychrome mosaic facing.

CASA BATLLÓ, 1904–06

Barcelona. View of interior entry hall and staircase with its exquisitely rendered bannister.

CASA BATLLÓ

View of the richly ornamented chimneys and the playful roof ridge.

ARCHES

Stone arches in Barcelona.

CASA MILÁ, 1906–10

Abstracted chimney on the roof of this Barcelona landmark.

PARK GÜELL, 1900–1914

Barcelona. Portion of the richly ornamented wall-bench encircling the open plaza on the roof of the "Hall of the Hundred Columns".

SAGRADA FAMILIA

Sculptural ensemble, Nativity Façade.

CASA MILÁ

Rooftop elements (stairway entrances) dressed in fragmented marble tiling.

CASA BATLLÓ

Façade detail of the ivory-coloured balustrades and heavily abstracted ceramic cladding which increases in density towards the top of the building.

BISHOP'S PALACE, 1887–93

Situated at Astorga, north-west Spain. The original scheme for the building was left incomplete by Gaudí at the death of the Bishop in 1893. The structure is remarkable for its strongly Neo-Gothic styling, and its use of white granite.

SAGRADA FAMILIA

Gaudi's most famous and controversial work. The spires (right) of the cathedral, display the textual references "Hosanna" and "Excelsis" embedded within the surface ornamentation.

SAGRADA FAMILIA

LEFT: The Sagrada Familia viewed from an oblique angle beneath an assembly of towers.

RIGHT: Nave of the eastern transept, the Nativity Façade, showing the scale of the apse cavity.

SAGRADA FAMILIA

Nativity Façade, Portal of Love, showing a sculptural depiction of the Coronation of the Virgin.

SAGRADA FAMILIA

LEFT: detail of one of the attendant figures populating the narrative portals of the Nativity Façade.

RIGHT: Sculptural detail of the Nativity Façade, depicting a dove.

SAGRADA FAMILIA

LEFT: Interior of one of the towers, showing the structural arrangement of the parabolic arches.

RIGHT: Exterior of the bell towers, inside of which is a stairway chamber.

COLEGIO TERESIANO 1888–89

High parabolic arches gives the interior galleries an austere and meditative atmosphere appropriate to the building.

GÜELL PALACE, 1886–89

Roof chimneys and ventilators give a strong sculptural presence.

INTERIOR, GÜELL PALACE

The sophisticated decorative ensemble was designed to impress, and exhibits a rich diversity of materials including marble, ironwork and wood, all treated with an impressive standard of hand craftsmanship.

GÜELL COLONY CRYPT, 1898–1917

Situated in Santa Coloma de Cervelló, outside Barcelona. The forecourt arcade shows the rich, mosaic-like combination of materials, colours and textures. The interior ceiling of the crypt, (right) shows a web of unstuccoed brick arches giving a deceptive impression of lightness and simplicity to this subterranean space.

CASA VICENS, 1883–88

Calle les Carolines, Barcelona. LEFT: Decorative ironwork is effectively integrated with a diversity of materials.
RIGHT: The pronounced *Mudejar* Influence is apparent in architectural forms and the sophisticated use of tile patterning and polychromy.

CASA VICENS

Detail of the interiors where the intricate dialogue of textures and materials speaks unequivocally of the Moorish influence. The delicacy of organic decorative motifs may also suggest the influence of the Arts and Crafts movement.

CASA "EL CAPRICHO", 1883–85

Situated in Comillas, near Santander in northern Spain. Designed without Gaudí ever having visited the site, this whimsical house boasts an eclectic combination of structural and decorative devices.

DRAGON GATE, GÜELL PAVILIONS, 1884–87

The formal entrance to the a Güell Pavilions in Barcelona. With its exquisite manipulation of materials, writhing curvilinear forms, the gate is considered an early example of Gaudí's use of an Art Nouveau decorative vocabulary.

PARK GÜELL

Tower adorned with spire and cross, Service Pavilion, at the main entryway to the park.

PARK GÜELL

The Caretaker's Lodge with its fantastic mosaic roofline silhouetted against the panorama of Barcelona below.

PARK GÜELL

LEFT: View of the park's main entrance gate at Carrer d'Olot.
RIGHT: Staircase leading to the so-called "Hall of the Hundred Columns", defended by the giant tile-encrusted lizard. The heavy Doric-inspired columns elevate an open plaza above.

PARK GÜELL

TOP LEFT: The park's defending lizard.
OTHER IMAGES: Decorative mosaics embellished with broken ceramic tiles, set into the enclosing perimeter wall two of which display the name of the park and commemorate the patron.

PARK GÜELL

LEFT: Interior arcade of parabolic-like arches.

RIGHT: View from below of the inner ceiling of the Doric arcade. One of a series of mosaic medallions (c.1909) by Gaudí's collaborator Josep Maria Jujol.

CASA BATTLÓ

LEFT: The undulating façade of polished Montjuïc stone.

RIGHT: Ceramic fireplace in the Batlló private apartments (top), and ground floor staircase leading to the quarters above. The balustrade displays a fossil-like derivation.

CASA BATTLÓ

LEFT: Detail of the first floor façade and upper balconies.

RIGHT: Inner courtyard faced with diverse hues of blue and white tiling.

CASA MILÁ

Situated at Passeig de Gràcia and Calle de Provença, Barcelona. Also known as "La Pedrera" (the "Quarry"), this shows the street elevation and three principal façades of the asymmetrical site.

CASA MILÁ

LEFT: Abstracted "helmeted heads" of warrior-chimneys on the rooftop.

RIGHT: Balconies featuring the intricate ironwork railings designed and executed in collaboration with Josep Maria Jujol.

Picture credits

The publishers would like to thank the following sources for their kind permission to reproduce the pictures in this book:

Arcaid/John Edward Linden 32, 75bl/Prisma 38, 39, 76
Architectural Association/Peter Barefoot 52, 53, 77bl
Corbis/O. Alamany & E. Vicens 66, 70, 71, 72, 79, 79tr/Peter Aprahamian 42, 50, 51, 69, 76bl, 77br, 79cl/Macduff Everton 2, 3, 74tr/Marc Garanger 58, 59, 78cl/Martin Jones 73, 79bl/Charles & Josette Lenars 7, 26, 47, 54, 55, 62t, 74br, 75, 77tr, 78tl/Ramon Manent 5, 46, 68, 74, 77tr, 79cl/Hans Georg Roth 30, 75br/Charles E. Rotkin 35, 76tl/Francesco Venturi; Kea Publishing Services 4, 48, 49, 74, 77cl/Patrick Ward 1, 12, 34, 36, 37, 61, 62b, 63, 65, 74tl, 75tl, 76tl, 76tr, 78, 79tl/K.M. Westermann 67, 79tr/Nik Wheeler 33, 60, 75bl, 78br/Adam Woolfitt 8,9, 40, 43, 44, 45, 74bl, 76br, 76bl, 77tl/ Michael S. Yamashita 64, 79tl
James Davis Travel Photography 56, 57, 78tr
Eye Ubiqitous/Larry Bray 20, 75tr/Linda Miles 41, 76

Every effort has been made to acknowledge correctly and contact the source and/copyright holder of each picture, and Carlton Books Limited apologises for any unintentional errors or omissions which will be corrected in future editions of this book.

Further reading

Güell, X, *Antoni Gaudí*, (Barcelona, 1986)

Howard, J., *Art Nouveau. International and National Styles in Europe*, (Manchester, 1996)

Kent, C. & D. Prindle, *Park Güell*, (New York, 1993)

Lahuerta, J., ed., *Gaudí*, (Barcelona, 1993)

Martinell, C., *Gaudí: His Life, His Theories, His Work*, (Cambridge, Mass., 1975)

Solê-Morales, I., *Fin-de-siècle Architecture in Barcelona*, (Barcelona, 1992)

Zerbst, R, *Antoni Gaudí*, (Cologne, 1993)